How & Why Spiders Spin Silk

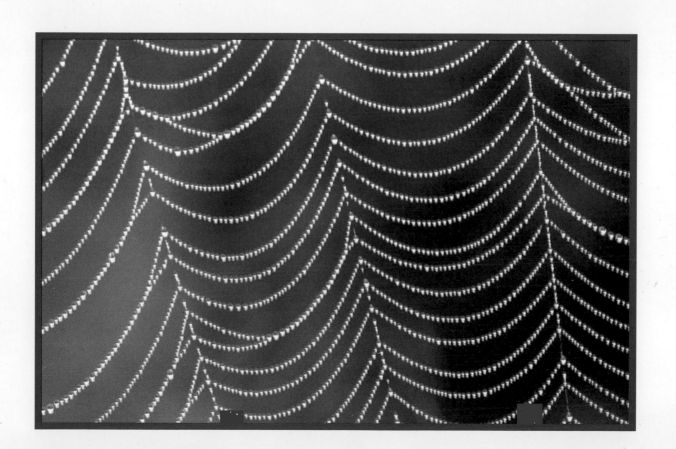

P9-DMB-525

A garden spider weaves a silky web. Covered with dew, the web looks like a diamond necklace.

A jumping spider spins a silk anchor line. The thread looks fragile, but it is very strong. Spiders make many kinds of silk. They use their silk in many ways.

A garden spider's web is a deadly insect trap. When a grasshopper blunders into the web, it is caught in the sticky silk threads. The hungry spider rushes over. It wraps its grasshopper meal in sheets of silk.

The silk is made by glands in the spider's belly. It comes out through openings called spinnerets. All spiders have spinnerets, and they all make silk this way.

The jumping spider pounces on its prey like a cat. As the spider leaps, its silk anchor line trails behind it. The silk is liquid when it comes out, but it dries at once.

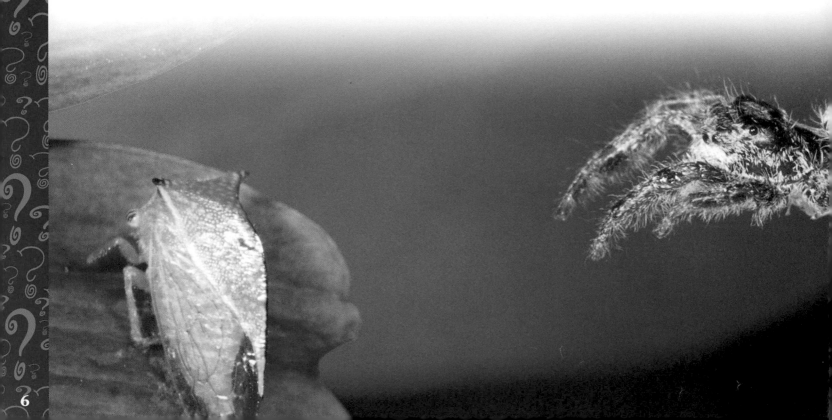

The anchor line is stronger than steel wire. It is firmly fastened to a flower. If the spider misses its mark, it will not fall very far. The anchor line will catch it. Then the spider will climb back up the anchor line to the flower.

Many spiders use silk to make nests. A silky nest is a safe place for a spider to hide.

You may have seen a house spider's nest. There may be one in your house! This spider's nest is a messy tangle of silk. The house spider is not a very neat housekeeper!

The crab spider has no web. It waits for insects to come to a flower. When a bee comes looking for nectar, the crab spider rushes out and bites it. The bite is poisonous, and the bee stops moving.

Then the spider pumps juices into the bee. The juices turn the inside of the bee into bee soup, and the spider sucks it up. The crab spider does not use silk to catch its prey. But like many spiders, it has other uses for silk.

Female spiders wrap their eggs in sheets of soft silk. Then the spider bundles her silk-wrapped eggs into a round egg sac. Many spiders stay near their eggs to guard them.

The wolf spider's egg sac is attached to her spinnerets.
She carries it wherever she goes.

The garden spider uses strong strands of silk to fasten her egg sac to a plant. Her eggs will spend the winter there, safe in their silky case.

Young spiders hatch inside the nest. In early spring, they leave the nest, ready to spin webs of their own.

Use the information in this book to answer some "how and why" questions.

- Why does a garden spider make a silk web?

- How does the spider make silk?

- How does silk keep a jumping spider from falling?

- How does the crab spider catch its prey?

- Why do spiders build nests?

- How do spiders use silk to protect their eggs?